D0710736

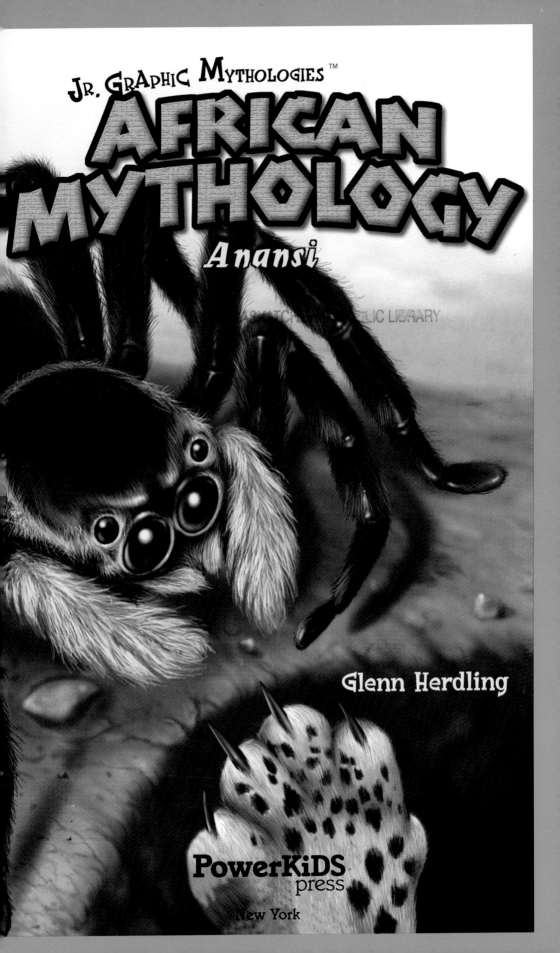

Jr. Graphic Mythologies™
AFRICAN MYTHOLOGY
Anansi

Glenn Herdling

PowerKiDS
press.

New York

Published in 2007 by The Rosen Publishing Group, Inc.
29 East 21st Street, New York, NY 10010

Copyright © 2007 by The Rosen Publishing Group, Inc.

First Edition

Editors: Daryl Heller and Julia Wong
Book Design: Greg Tucker
Illustrations: Q2A

Library of Congress Cataloging-in-Publication Data

Herdling, Glenn.
  African mythology : Anansi / by Glenn Herdling.— 1st ed.
    p. cm. — (Jr. graphic mythologies)
  Includes index.
  ISBN (10) 1-4042-3398-9 — (13) 978-1-4042-3398-0 (lib. bdg.) —
ISBN (10) 1-4042-2151-4 — (13) 978-1-4042-2151-2 (pbk.)
  1. Anansi (Legendary character)—Legends. 2. Tales—Africa. 3. Mythology, African.
I. Title. II. Series.
  GR75.A64A43 2007
  398.2096'0452544—dc22

                                        2006002786

Manufactured in the United States of America

CONTENTS

MAJOR CHARACTERS

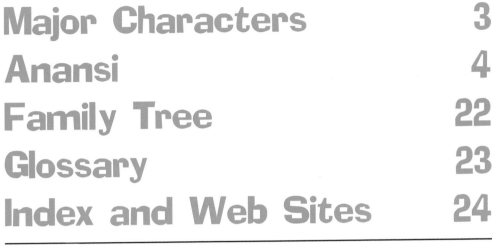

Kwaku Anansi *(KWAH-koo a-NAHN-see) was the first spider. He was very smart and could trick other animals. Anansi was married to Mistress Anansi. He created the Sun, the Moon, and the stars. He also taught humans how to farm.*

Nyame *(NYAH-meh) was the god of the sky. He was the father of Anansi. He was also the owner of all the world's stories until Anansi won the stories from him.*

Onini *(oh-NEE-nee) was a python, or large snake. Pythons live in Africa, Asia, and Australia. Some pythons grow to be 10 feet (3 m) long. Onini was one of the animals that Anansi captured.*

Osebo *(oh-SAY-boh) was a leopard, or large cat. Leopards live in Africa and Asia. They usually sleep during the day and hunt at night. Osebo was one of the animals that Anansi captured.*

ANANSI

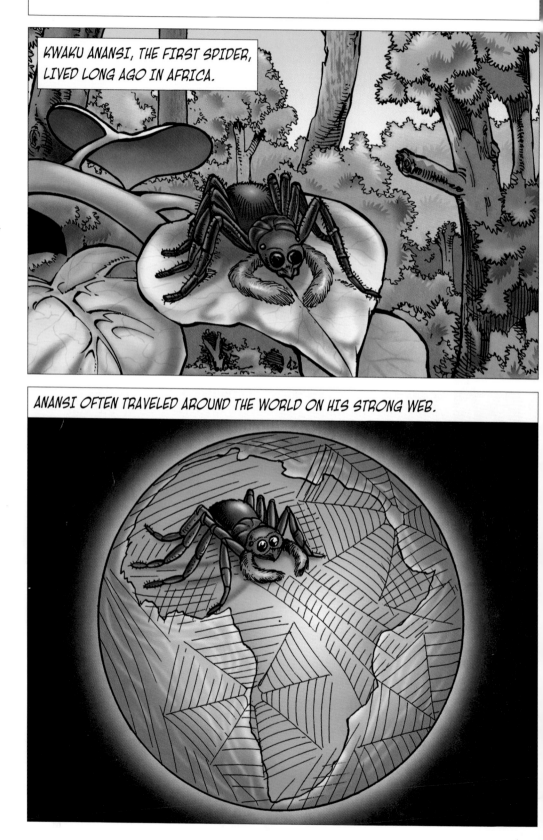

KWAKU ANANSI, THE FIRST SPIDER, LIVED LONG AGO IN AFRICA.

ANANSI OFTEN TRAVELED AROUND THE WORLD ON HIS STRONG WEB.

IN THOSE DAYS THERE WERE NO STORIES FOR ANYONE TO TELL. NYAME, THE SKY GOD, KEPT THEM LOCKED IN A BOX.

ANANSI WANTED TO OWN THE WORLD'S STORIES SO HE COULD KNOW THE BEGINNINGS AND ENDINGS OF THINGS.

ANANSI DECIDED TO VISIT NYAME IN HIS **KINGDOM** HIGH ABOVE THE CLOUDS.

NYAME SAID HIS PRICE WAS TO CAPTURE THREE CREATURES. THEY WERE MMOBORO, THE **STINGING HORNETS**, ONINI, THE HUNGRY PYTHON, AND OSEBO, THE CLAWING LEOPARD.

ANANSI CARRIED THE GOURD AND A BOWL FILLED WITH WATER THROUGH THE FOREST.
HE STOPPED WHEN HE FOUND THE STINGING HORNETS.

ANANSI SPLASHED HIMSELF
WITH SOME OF THE WATER.

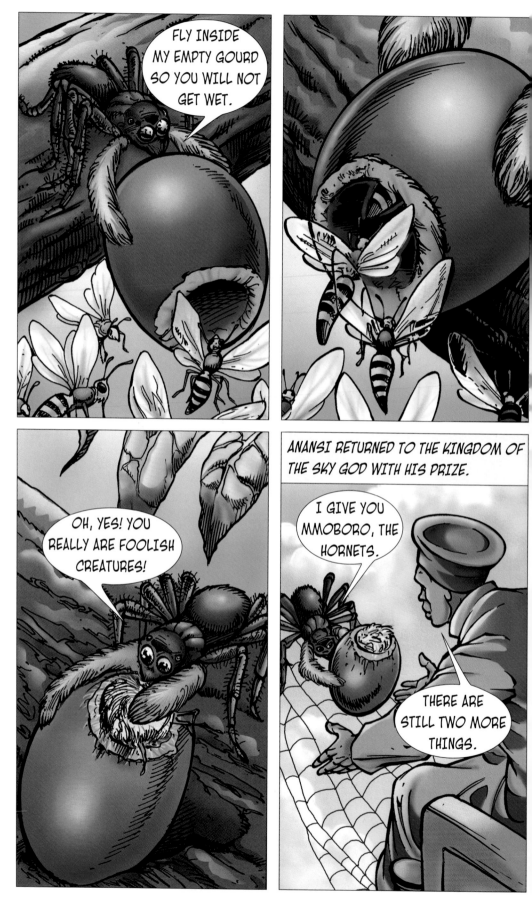

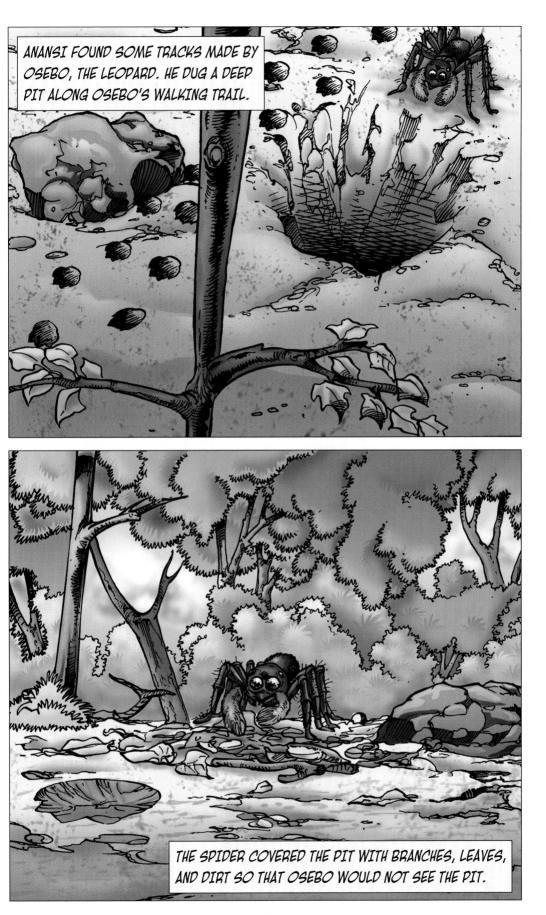

ANANSI FOUND SOME TRACKS MADE BY OSEBO, THE LEOPARD. HE DUG A DEEP PIT ALONG OSEBO'S WALKING TRAIL.

THE SPIDER COVERED THE PIT WITH BRANCHES, LEAVES, AND DIRT SO THAT OSEBO WOULD NOT SEE THE PIT.

WHEN THE TRAP WAS FINISHED, ANANSI LEFT FOR THE NIGHT. SOON AFTER, OSEBO CAME **PROWLING** FOR FOOD.

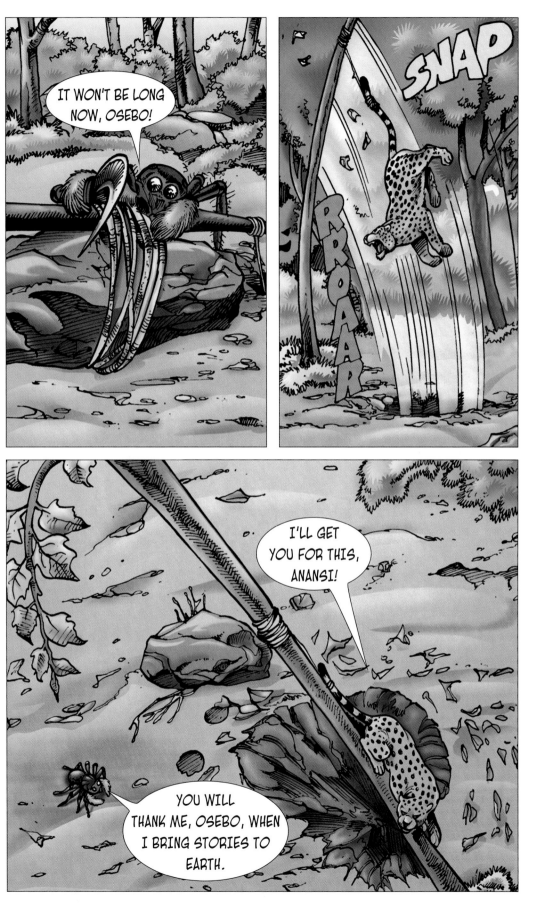

ANANSI AND HIS WIFE WERE HAPPY TO LEARN EACH AND EVERY STORY.

TODAY, ANANSI'S MANY WEBS ARE **PROOF** THAT HE IS STILL SPINNING HIS TALES FOR ALL TO SHARE.

THE END

FAMILY TREE

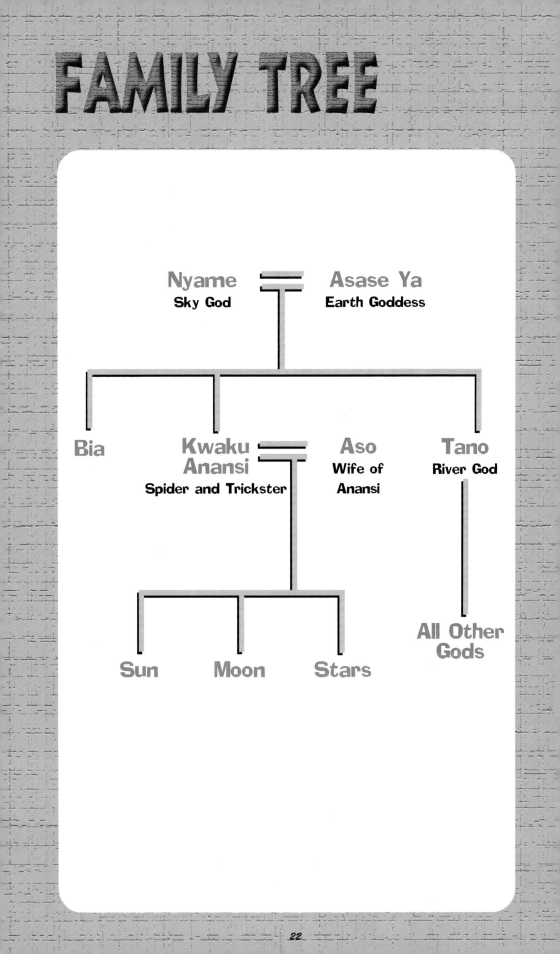

Nyame — **Asase Ya**
Sky God — Earth Goddess

Bia

Kwaku Anansi — **Aso**
Spider and Trickster — Wife of Anansi

Tano
River God

Sun **Moon** **Stars**

All Other Gods

GLOSSARY

bamboo (bam-BOO) A thick, woody grass with hollow stems that is used to make huts and furniture.

gourd (GORD) A round fruit from a vine, whose hard shell is used to make bowls.

hornets (HOR-nets) Large, flying insects that have a stinger.

kingdom (KING-dum) An area or territory headed by a king.

prisoner (PRIZ-ner) Something that has lost its freedom.

proof (PROOF) Something that shows that something is true.

prowling (PROWL-ing) Moving about as if in search of animals to eat.

stinging (STING-ing) Pricking with poison.

stretch (STRECH) To make longer.

vine (VYN) A plant with a long stem that climbs around objects or creeps along the ground.

warriors (WAR-yurz) People who fight in a war.

INDEX

WEB SITES

Due to the changing nature of Internet links, PowerKids Press has developed an online list of Web sites related to the subject of this book. This site is updated regularly. Please use this link to access the list:
www.powerkidslinks.com/myth/anansi/